CCSS **Genre** Realistic Fi...

 Essential Question
In what ways can you help your community?

Playground Buddy

by Paul Mason
illustrated by
Gabrielle Grimard

Chapter 1
"Any Volunteers?" 2

Chapter 2
Duty First. 5

Chapter 3
Here to Help. 8

Chapter 4
A Big Thanks 12

Respond to Reading 16

PAIRED READ **Making a Difference** 17

Focus on Literary Elements 20

Chapter 1 "Any Volunteers?"

"I have exciting news," announced Mrs. Wilder one morning. "The school is looking for volunteers to train as playground buddies."

Sofia looked up from her drawing and waited for her teacher to tell them more.

"Playground buddies are trained to help other kids deal with problems in school," explained Mrs. Wilder. "Is anyone interested?"

Sofia's hand shot into the air. She enjoyed helping other kids. She glanced hopefully at her friend Jade, but Jade shook her head to show she wasn't interested.

"That's great, Sofia!" Mrs. Wilder said, smiling. "They want mature fifth graders like you. You'll be assigned two lunchtimes a week to patrol the playground. You get to wear a special yellow vest so people know who to talk to. Are there any more volunteers?"

Sofia gave Jade another pleading look, but she didn't notice. Over in the corner, Tim raised his hand.

"Wonderful, Tim," said Mrs. Wilder. "Thank you both for your generosity. Trust me, you'll enjoy it. The training begins tomorrow—listen to the morning announcements."

The next day, Sofia waited impatiently all morning for the buddy training to begin.

At lunchtime the volunteers met in the library. The trainer, Jim, was waiting for them. Sofia could see Jade and the others playing four square on the playground.

Jim passed around some brochures. "Organizations like ours bring the buddy program into schools all over the country," he told them. "We're selective about who we train because it's such an important job."

Jim explained that being a buddy meant being there for someone who needs a friend. "You're there to listen and help, and that's really important," he said.

The training was interesting and fun. Sofia was excited.

STOP AND CHECK

What do playground buddies do?

Sofia collected her vest from the library and quickly got ready. It was her first buddy duty since the training. It felt good to be wearing the vest, but she was also a little nervous.

The sun was shining, and everyone was outside, scattered around the playground. Sofia skirted the edge of the basketball courts, trying to spot anyone who looked like they needed help.

Jade and some of the others ran up to her. "Hey, buddy," said Jade with a smile. "We're going to play soccer. Are you coming?"

Sofia looked at the kids running around, having fun. She hesitated, then she shook her head. "I can't, guys. I'd like to, but I'm on buddy duty. Tomorrow?" she asked hopefully.

"I guess we could play some other time," said Jade, disappointed, as they left.

STOP AND CHECK

How does Sofia feel about being a playground buddy?

Chapter 3 Here to Help

Sofia sighed as she watched the rest of the school laughing and playing games. Then she walked around the edge of the playground again and saw a young girl sitting all alone.

Sofia went over to the girl. Her knees were bunched up, and her face was buried in her legs. Sofia remembered the lines they had practiced in training.

"Hi, I'm Sofia," she said gingerly. "I'm a playground buddy, and I'm here to help."

The little girl looked up, and Sofia recognized her as a new girl in first grade. "Why don't you tell me what's wrong. It might make you feel better," Sofia said.

The girl looked at Sofia's vest and nodded. "My name's Kim," she said, wiping her eyes.

Sofia offered her hand. "Why don't we take a walk around the playground."

The two of them walked for a while, not really going anywhere, just wandering. Sofia waited for Kim to find her voice.

"I'm the only new kid in my whole class," Kim said finally. "I'm all alone," she sniffed.

Sofia listened as Kim told her that she liked her teacher, who was really nice, but at recess and lunchtime, she felt lost and lonely. It seemed like no one wanted to play with her.

They walked by the four-square court. "How about joining in a game?" suggested Sofia. "Come on, it'll be fun."

Kim hung back, feeling shy. Sofia called one of the players over. "Aida, can Kim join your game? She's new, and I know you're a great friend."

Aida smiled. "Sure," she said. "Come on, Kim!"

The next day at
lunchtime, Sofia looked
around for Kim. She
didn't have to look
too hard. Her little
buddy ran up, holding
hands with Aida.

"Hi, Kim," said
Sofia, laughing. "I see
you have a friend now."

"Yes, this is Aida.
She's in first grade, too."

"Thanks for being my buddy, Sofia,"
said Kim.

"You're welcome, Kim."

As Kim and Aida ran off together, Sofia
was glad to see Kim smiling. Her buddy was
coming out of her shell.

STOP AND CHECK

How does Sofia
help Kim?

Chapter 4 A Big Thanks

Sofia found herself pretty busy during her next buddy duty. She helped end an argument over a ball, found a lost shoe, and suggested a better way of sharing the slide.

"Maybe I should have said yes when Mrs. Wilder asked for volunteers," said Jade after watching Sofia help someone. "Being a playground buddy is kind of cool."

"You can still be one," Sofia replied with a smile. "There's another training day soon."

Just then, she heard Mrs. Wilder calling, "Sofia!" She was outside the office with a woman Sofia didn't know.

Sofia left Jade and ran over. She wondered if there was a problem. But both women were smiling.

"This is Mrs. Chen, Kim's mother," said Mrs. Wilder.

"Hello, Sofia. I won't take up too much of your time. I can see you're busy," said Mrs. Chen, pointing at Sofia's vest. "I just wanted to thank you for helping Kim. She found it hard changing schools, and she was miserable."

Mrs. Chen smiled. "Now Kim can't wait to get to school. It's all because you helped her find a friend."

Sofia blushed. "I'm glad I could help."

"Students like you make new residents like us feel welcome," Mrs. Chen said. "We're really grateful."

"You're welcome," Sofia said quietly.

"Smile!" Mrs. Wilder whispered into Sofia's ear as they left. "You did well!"

Sofia skipped back to the playground. Mrs. Wilder was right. She had done well. And that made her feel good. She'd have to remember to volunteer more often.

STOP AND CHECK

Why does Mrs. Chen feel grateful?

Respond to Reading

Use important details from *Playground Buddy* to summarize the story. Your graphic organizer may help.

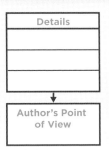

Details

↓

Author's Point of View

Text Evidence

1. How can you tell that *Playground Buddy* is realistic fiction? **GENRE**

2. Is this story told by a first-person or third-person narrator? Use examples from the text to tell about the narrator's point of view. **POINT OF VIEW**

3. What does *skirted* on page 5 mean? Use clues in the sentence to help you figure out the meaning. **DEFINITIONS AND RESTATEMENTS**

4. Write about how the narrator's point of view helps you understand each character in this story. **WRITE ABOUT READING**

Compare Texts

Read about another volunteer who helps people in the community.

Making a Difference

"To be a leader, you must be a reader!"

That's the slogan of a charity in Moraga, California, that provides free books to people in need.

The charity began in 1999. It has given away thousands of books and educational materials. The books and materials often replace resources lost in natural disasters such as hurricanes and earthquakes.

The charity relies on volunteers—people who work for no pay. Jennifer Tao is one of those volunteers.

Jennifer Tao says that volunteering "makes you feel really fulfilled by sharing your time and helping other people."

Cynthia Brian

Jennifer Tao started working for the charity when she was just 14. Later she led the Operation Hurricane Relief project. The project delivered around $27,000 worth of books and other resources to the Gulf Coast after Hurricane Katrina in 2005.

Jennifer helped to raise money for the charity. When she heard about a grant from the National Education Association, she decided to apply for the grant.

Focus on Literary Elements

Dialogue Writers use quotation marks to show that a character is speaking. The speaker is usually shown by the use of *said* and their name.

Read and Find In this sentence you know right away that Sofia is speaking: "It might make you feel better," Sofia said. (page 8)

Using the context of a sentence can help you figure out who is speaking: "You're welcome, Kim." (page 11) You can figure out that Sofia is speaking because the sentence before the dialogue refers to her.

Using a different verb can tell you how the character spoke: "I have exciting news," announced Mrs. Wilder one morning. (page 2)

Your Turn

Copy this chart. With a partner, look for examples in the story of the different ways that dialogue is written. Fill in the chart with the examples you find.

Dialogue	Example
Using *said*	
Using the sentence context	
Using a verb other than *said*	

Grants are donations of money that charities try to win. Winning a grant isn't easy, because many charities usually apply. Jennifer had never done it before, but she took on the challenge—and won the grant, first time.

Many people like Jennifer volunteer as fund-raisers. Do you know someone who raises money for a charity?

Top Volunteer Activities (2008–2010)

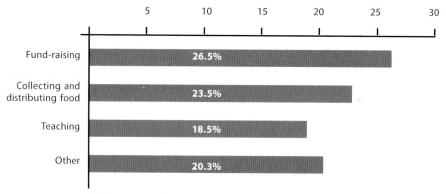

This graph shows the kind of work volunteers do across the United States.

Make Connections

How does the charity Jennifer works for help communities? ESSENTIAL QUESTION

What do Sofia in *Playground Buddy* and Jennifer in *Making a Difference* enjoy about their volunteer work? TEXT TO TEXT